The ANTARCTIC versus the ARCTIC

D0541378

Contents

1.	The Arctic	5
2.	The Antarctic	17
	Questions	31
	Index	32

Badger
LEARNING

Vocabulary

accidentally

communicate

antlers

continent

blubber

enemies

camouflage

orbiting

1. The ARCTIC

The Arctic is the area around the North Pole. The pole itself isn't on land, it is on ice formed by the frozen sea.

There are eight countries in the Arctic:

- USA
- Greenland
- Canada
- Norway
- Sweden
- Finland
- Russia

and a very small part of Iceland.

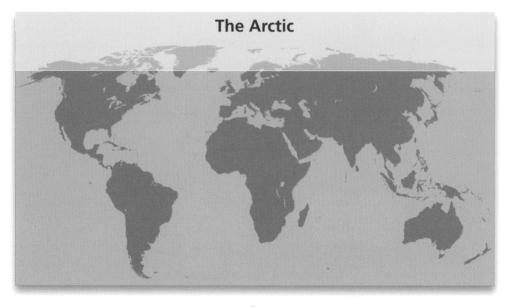

The Arctic

People often think that
the Arctic is just ice and
snow. But it is not. It also
has millions of trees.

WOW! facts

The Arctic Ocean is massive.
It covers over six million square miles.

Animals all over the world have coats that camouflage them so they cannot be seen.

Animals that live in the snow also need to be camouflaged so they have white coats.

Snowy owls have white feathers so they cannot be seen by their prey. They hunt during the day and at night.

They use their strong talons to catch small animals such as lemmings.

In the Arctic winter some small animals live under the snow to shelter from the weather and hide from their enemies.

Lemmings are small rodents, like rats. They build tunnels under the snow that are many metres long.

Lemmings have very sharp teeth, which they use to gnaw through roots of plants growing above ground.

In winter, the fur of the Arctic fox is white, so it is well-camouflaged to hide itself from polar bears or wolves. But in the summer, when some parts of the Arctic snow melt, the fox's fur changes colour to grey to blend in with the background.

WOW! facts

The Arctic fox can hear its prey under the thick snow. It jumps in the air and breaks through the layer of snow to get to its next meal.

Some Arctic wolves have white fur and some have grey or black fur. The fur is very thick and it keeps them warm during the cold winters.

Wolves live in packs and communicate by howling.

The pack works together to attack big animals, such as reindeer. Wolves have an excellent sense of smell and can smell other animals from a mile away.

Polar bears are the biggest land hunters on Earth.

They walk around 20,000 kilometres every year and can swim very long distances. Polar bears have long hairs on the soles of their feet, which keep out the cold and stop them slipping on ice.

A polar bear is so strong it can kill an animal with one blow from its paw.

WOW! facts

Polar bear fur is not white!
It is actually clear, but looks white because it reflects light, just like snow.

The bearded seal gets its name because of the whiskers on its face.

It is the biggest type of seal in the Arctic, and can weigh up to 240 kilograms. Most of this weight is a thick layer of blubber to keep it warm.

Even though they are big, seals are the favourite food of polar bears.

WOW! facts

The polar bear waits by a hole in the ice for a seal to come up for air. Then the polar bear grabs the seal's head and flips it onto the ice.

Reindeer are the only deer in the world whose males and females both have antlers.

Reindeer antlers are like a human's fingerprint. No two reindeer antlers are exactly the same.

Reindeer live in large herds of up to one million deer. They are quick movers! They can run at 50 miles per hour!

Gyrfalcons are the biggest falcons in the world.

From tip to tip their wings can be 122 centimetres.

They mainly eat birds. Gyrfalcons can catch birds as large as a goose. When hunting, a gyrfalcon can fly at more than 125 miles per hour.

They can fly so fast they just overtake other birds and snatch them out of the sky.

Arctic hares are not much like a cuddly pet rabbit.

They can grow to more than 60 centimetres long and weigh six kilograms. On very cold days, they gather in groups and huddle together to keep warm.

However, they don't always get along with each other. The males have been known to stand on their back legs, and box and scratch at each other to impress females during the mating season.

Musk ox eat grass and plants. In winter they dig through the snow with their feet to reach food.

They have the longest hair of any animal in the world.

Every year when the male musk oxen try to impress females, they charge at each other and clash heads together. Luckily they have an air pocket between their brain and skull to prevent brain damage.

2. The ANTARCTIC

The Antarctic is the area around the South Pole.

The pole is on land that is covered by a layer of ice that is two kilometres deep.

This is the coldest, driest and windiest continent on Earth. The Antarctic is a desert as it hardly ever snows or rains this far south.

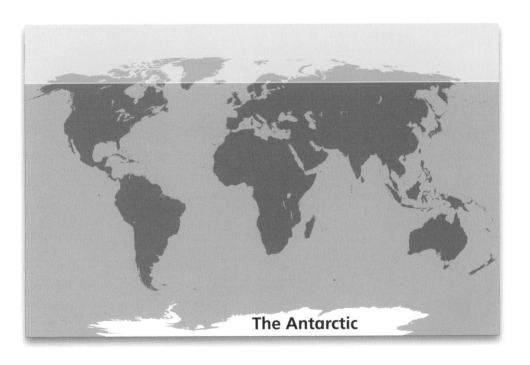

The Antarctic

Grass and trees do not grow in the Antarctic. Animals get their food from the water.

Krill are tiny sea creatures that look like shrimps. They are eaten by almost everything that lives in the Antarctic.

Krill live in swarms so big that they can be seen from orbiting spacecraft.

WOW! facts

Even though a krill is only the size of your little finger the total weight of all Antarctic krill is more than the total weight of all humans on Earth!

Although penguins have small wings, they can't fly. Their wings are used for swimming underwater.

They move very fast in the water but not so fast when they waddle on land. So they often slide on their tummies over ice and snow to get around.

Penguins eat fish. A large penguin can collect up to 30 fish in one dive!

The first Antarctic explorers thought that penguins were fish that grew feathers. No-one believed that birds could survive in such terrible weather.

There are 20 million penguins in the Antarctic. Most live on the islands around the coast.

The emperor is the biggest species of penguin.

At the end of summer (February) most penguins move to warmer places.

In winter (May) female emperor penguins lay one egg. The temperature is -50°C.

An egg will freeze on the ice so the male penguin pushes it onto his feet.

He covers the egg with his stomach to keep it warm. The female goes to find food and the male stays to protect the egg.

He does not eat for ten weeks and loses nearly half his body weight.

Penguins have no enemies on the ice but in the sea they are chased by killer whales.

These huge hunters are the most dangerous animals in the Antarctic. They use their 50 ten-centimetre-long teeth to eat other whales, seals, fish and penguins.

Killer whales weigh ten tonnes and can swim up to 34 miles per hour.

WOW! facts

Killer whales kill sharks by holding them upside down underwater for 15 minutes.

Some leopard seals are more than three metres long.

They are powerful hunters and have long, sharp teeth. Their main food is penguins and smaller seals.

They grab hold of a penguin's feet, then take it to the surface and shake it to death before eating it.

They sometimes even attack people.

Elephant seal facts

These huge, ugly seals are the biggest seals in the Antarctic.

Male elephant seals can weigh four tonnes and can grow longer than an average car. The females are only half that size.

Elephant seals can hold their breath underwater for over an hour and a half!

When an elephant seal gets angry, its nose fills with air and looks like an elephant's trunk. That is how they got their name.

Wandering albatrosses have the longest wings of any bird. They can be three and a half metres long.

They fly more than five million kilometres during their life. One albatross flew all around the world in 46 days.

A young albatross is fed by its parents for nine months. It then flies away and does not come back to land for five years.

Snow petrels are the size of a pigeon. They have pure white feathers and black beaks and eyes.

They only live around the Antarctic. They nest closer to the South Pole than any other bird. They eat fish and krill.

WARNING!

Don't get too close to a snow petrel nest. They will squirt a disgusting stream of smelly sick at you!

The craziest thing about crabeater seals is that they don't eat crabs! Scientists accidentally gave them the wrong name. In fact, crabeater seals mainly eat krill.

They have amazing teeth that have hooks on each tooth and the top and bottom rows interlock. This helps them to filter krill from the water.

There are lots of crabeater seals around the Antarctic. Scientists reckon there are about 35 million.

Blue whales are the biggest animals on Earth. But they eat tiny krill. Each whale can swallow 40 million krill a day.

Whales are mammals and need to breathe air just like humans. A blue whale can hold its breath under water for half an hour. When it comes up and blows air out of its blowhole, it shoots up as tall as a three-storey building!

WOW! facts

A blue whale's blowhole is big enough for a baby to crawl into!

Questions

Name a country that is part of the Arctic. *(page 5)*

What colour is a polar bear's fur? *(page 11)*

Which is the biggest species of penguin in the world? *(page 21)*

How does the male penguin keep an egg warm? *(page 23)*

How fast can a killer whale swim? *(page 24)*

What does the blue whale eat? *(page 30)*

INDEX

albatrosses 27
Antarctic 17, 18, 21, 24, 26, 28-29
Arctic 5, 6, 8-9, 10,12,15
Arctic fox 9
Arctic hares 15
blowhole 30
blue whale 30, 31
camouflage 7
crabeater seals 29
hunters 11, 24
killer whales 24, 31
krill 18, 28, 29, 30
lemmings 7, 8
North Pole 5
penguins 19, 20, 21, 22, 24-25
polar bears 9, 11, 12
seals 12, 24, 25, 26, 29
snowy owls 7
South Pole 17, 28
wolves 9, 10